WESTERN STORM

YASHVEER VATS GAURAV

Made with ♥ on the Notion Press Platform
www.notionpress.com

To those who carried storms in their chests and still taught me what it means to breathe.

This book is for the friend who once promised they'd sit beside me if the world was ending, and for everyone who has ever loved with that same reckless sincerity. It is for the people who became mirrors when I could no longer recognize myself, and for the ones who left, teaching me that absence, too, has a voice, and sometimes it speaks louder than presence.

I dedicate these pages to my parents, who taught me patience, faith, and resilience even when I faltered. To my teachers, who gave me the courage to put words on paper. And to the cast of voices who stepped into my imagination and lent flesh to shadows—without you, Suraci's world would still be only silence.

But above all, this book belongs to you, the reader. For choosing to walk into the storm with me, for opening these pages and letting my flawed characters stumble into your mind. May you find pieces of yourself in their despair, and fragments of hope in their struggle.

Thank you

for keeping the promise still.

Contents

Contents

Contents

Contents

Preface

This book has been a journey, I will not lie when I say I've written this with the absolute rawness within my soul. It was supposed to be a normal Anthology, but I kept noticing patterns and thought "I can make something of this" and I did. I finally did.

The lore developed over time will be explained more in later books and blogs (@yvlosea is my Instagram).

I think we are all so used to this idea of the world being saved and saviours always being heroes or martyrs, This feeling of hopelessness that comes with being accountable for too much at a young age and losing bonds because of fatal flaws that don't come through us but societal pressure is explored in the book.

Suraci, for once wanted to be selfish and live for himself. but he was built to save others, he was built to be accountable to humans. There is a sense of dehumanisation I have put in Suraci's character, this dissonance of what he is.

Abandoned by his Goddess and abandoned by his best friend, his world crumbled as the two things he was made for were taken away from him with a snap of a finger,

Who could he blame? The world had ended and his best friend didn't fulfil the promise. The rage and Familiarity of Doom felt uncomfortable.

Suraci didn't take the guilt for the world ending, his guilt stemmed from the fact that he wasn't enough for his best friend to fight for him, or to complete his promise.

He was mad at Womb Goddess and Soileh, *but did he have the right to be?*

Acknowledgements

To everyone who helped me write this book, I especially want to thank the cast of Western Storm.

1.

Sara Shah As Moherani (@bipolarbegum)

2.

Sukriti Sinha As Vrakisorianna (@whisperinink)

3.

Saif Madre As Blacksmith of Bearing Bones (@Metaphorsandmuses)

4.

Priti Jha as Lilac Lady (@wickedwoid)

To my parents, who supported me throughout my journey, and assisted me through my writing.

To my teachers who helped me through this Literary journey.

Thank you Sanchita Ma'am, Mousami Ma'am, Shreya Ma'am, Shuchi Ma'am, Prisha Ma'am and Especially Suhani Ma'am.

Prologue

✦ The Core Lore

The world of Western Storm was once whole, bound together by divine order and mortal faith. Suraci, chosen by the Womb Goddess, was prophesied to prevent the apocalypse. But when he failed, the world splintered into five storm-ravaged lands:

Mist Hills – shrouded in fog, birthplace of myths and Suraci's first grace.

Disdain Town – a haunted settlement of decay, cynicism, and broken bonds.

Rage Lake – a place of fury and sacrifice, where gods' curses linger.

Lilac Sea – a surreal ocean infused with divine sorrow.

Repugnant Ruins – the fractured remnants of civilization, consumed by storms.

Now, the storm itself is eternal — both punishment and prison. Suraci wanders these lands, haunted by the promise broken by his best friend Soileh, and pursued by Moherani, the embodiment of death.

✦ Religions & Factions

The Womb Goddess & Her Cults

Goddess of creation and fate, who chose Suraci.

Revered as a giver of humanity yet feared for her indifference.

Followers practice rituals of servitude, believing suffering is divine will.

The Srishenti

Ancient tribe, first to taste ambrosia and learn divine flaws.

Cursed with madness, trapped in the land of death.

Half-revered, half-feared — embody both wisdom and decay.

The Covenant of Dawn

A cult praying for light in endless night.

They await a "second savior" to succeed where Suraci failed.

Obsessive rituals at sunrise, though the sun rarely pierces the storm.

Vraakasorriana (Warrior Nun Order)

Ageless order devoted to sacrifice and discipline.

Their faith teaches that suffering purifies the soul.

Vraakasorriana herself is a central figure tied to Suraci's path.

The Blacksmith of Bearing Bones (Taackkricoit)

A smith bound to divine fire, crafting with relics of the dead.

Represents the burden of service to gods without reward.

His followers see fire as both destruction and creation.

The Apostle of Apologies

A spectral entity embodying regret.

More philosophy than faction — those who follow it believe life itself must constantly atone.

Haunts Suraci as a mirror of his guilt.

Moherani (Death Incarnate)

The inevitable, eternal force chasing Suraci.

Seen by some as divine justice, by others as liberation.

Factions either worship Moherani as a goddess of endings, or curse her as the devourer.

Western Storm is not a battle of good versus evil, but a collision of flawed gods, broken promises, and human desperation to find meaning after the end of the world.

Would you like me to turn this into a reader-friendly appendix (so it can be added at the end of the book), or into a publisher's lore guide (more structured, like a reference bible)?

Mist Hills

Suraci ventures to the mist hills, the place where he met Soileh. Rethinking about the time when the world was still, and for the first time, he saw the womb goddess's grace. The value of life was visible, but it was unfair. it was a carrot hanging in front of a pig, the filthy pig being Suraci, The failing saviour of the compass.

The world had ended, and the world was divided into 4 Lands that didn't suffice for humanity and 90% of them were buried in the storm. No one could pass the storms, it was eternal damnation.

The Oldest tribe of ours was retaking the lands, the *Srishenti* were ancient people, the first to taste ambrosia, the first to figure out the flaws of the divine, the first to lose their sanity and be cursed to live in the land of death.

Suraci feels this indescribable unfairness of his servitude, he serves a goddess that puts him on a pedestal that crumbles to be a quartz landslide on humanity,

the end of the world because Suraci couldn't hold onto Soileh's hand forever, a curse bitten to the bones of this earth. but what could be worse? Soileh said "if the world was ending, I'd be right next to you" but he ended up being the reason the world collapsed. And no one knows.

To the living World, Suraci is a lost hero

To Suraci's World, he's not worth the comfort you'd need when the world
ends.

*Because Suraci is a Suraci, a slave to the goddess, a pawn to the fates. How
could he ever have a happy ending? he wasn't human enough, just hero enough
to be a failure.*

1. Made

The womb Goddess Crafted me with her own twenty tinctures, She built and ripped my soul a billion times before I could be born into this Ancient trope of contemporary suffering. She beaded my heart with plots of those who could never love me back and tainted my skin the shade of silver, the shade better than others and still never enough. She promised me a land of humanity. She knew my fondness of the humane and gave me the sparks to let me delve into this, this humanity she knew I could never be a part of. She gave me skin and bones and a spirit unlike anyone else, she gave me everything, and I still complain. But no matter how much humanity she'd spill through, I would never be able to contain it. I am not built for humanity, I am a starving star fed up on runes trying to devour meat like its my death row meal. I'm a spoilt machine, given the ability to grieve. Too much to be a human but too less for anything else to be. Craving the favor of being accepted as the savior or the flavor of being isolated enough to never be seen. Made me a poet, made me a queen, never made me enough to be a god or a human being. Dwindling on the sanity of being some amalgamation of an abrasive feel.

2. Messiah

The sun had sunk, and as I glanced over to the flames where you sat. and I sifted my hand through your hair like weaving silk.

The careful little sparks of your eyes liked my weaving, you counted my fingers, then the knots of your curled hair. Until we had words to talk with rather than the numbering of my actions.

And we mumbled and fumbled on our feet on the hills of niche names. You were so lost in the woods and I was so lost in you. But a part of me said it went both ways. being lost, or perhaps a part of me was warning me about what I was about to lose.

For a moment, I felt my feathers clash with your wings. I did not notice the fragility you carried with your soul, how the weight of shame resisted you from gliding through the sky we could've conquered.

So I held your hand, and you gave me a silver ring. said it was a pact, And sirens blared the valleys we had our letters engraved in, the trees. the silver ring didn't mean anything much to you, so on our way back from the land of history. you took the ring back, You took my heart right off my chest. made a crescent void.

But you sat beside me, stared at the moon, Said it's pretty at the same time as me. and then you looked at me Like I was the son of the god. Like the messiah. A messiah with a crescent in his chest.

And I landed back in the place of nowhere, Where I wanted to be was disdain town. I wanted to be in the same haunted town as you. But I was pulled to the distance by the gods.

and in the markets of the distance, I found silver rings. And lilac worns. and I thought to myself. what is love if not mimicry, The urge to become your lover, to become the same entity. Absolute convergence.

The moon waned its crescent to haunt the street I wanted to Walk, the one I had been resisting for a few long hours. The one in disdain town, The one I was separated from by the gods.

Fate had tied its strings around the rings that I acquired at the unknown lands. And she had her wrath set to burn down the fingers these rings would land on. And I had the gist, The gist of pessimism.

The way it was all doomed, me and happiness were at war since my birth. All fate had to do was create an impossible prophecy that would haunt my dreams for the next decade, if I lived past it all.

But no. I had to slim away the slammer of pessimism. There had to be a reason, Maybe redemption? life would finally apologize. And clementine was it

I believe it. With my hands cold-bleeding my soul as clench my chest hoping the crescent will heal and I'll harvest my redemption like the flavour of more survival, the flavour of hope.

I think about you, in the essence of how you're the kindest world has been to me.

Will you be my armistice, Or will just be another sword that shatters in the war?

The heavy gilded glass you wear disguised as golden armour, knowing you cannot lift the gold, and the glass is delicate, one crack and your skin will be barbed, and no blanket could heal it.

But you have bangles of gold, you have a heart I cannot see. You're made of my

incoherently crafted destiny. You have already taken a piece of me.

But it's okay, I am not one to complain about your flaws, The way your faults entice me to hold your hand as you walk through the seabed. We are both young, We are both Living, and we will both learn. I will walk on fire, and let you complain about the itchy grass.

It's a fool's world, and I'm a poet and you're a soldier not bloomed yet. either the gilded glass will turn into gold, or it'll crack and turn you into a fool. you're a

promised land, you're a legacy. And I watch in horror, with the glass half empty, thinking if you'll live through my ghouls.

The continuity haunted me, The strings of fate whirled around my neck like a leash to the deathless gods of misery, and how they leached back to my shoulder like the day we sat for 9 hours on bus seats.

But honouring our time together was not enough. I needed to make a temple on our existence, I needed the pillars engraved in braille for the blind to find solace that love is incomprehensible and still existent. I'd build us idols, but you cannot be captured into a sculpture.

I'd engrave the pillar with the words we lacked, write poems about how it felt, how the sunrise became an event I couldn't go without seeing, so I fostered the world in your eyes. How starlight was not visible through our city so I promised to look at you with the hope that kills tragedies. You looked at me with the sunrise in your eyes and I was the moon,

And you said you loved me, more than you've loved anyone. Across the skies and stars. You said I was the closest you've been to a human being. I was everything.

There was a brief time, when I said there was nothing to be liked about me, In the end. The curse of my depth is stronger than anyone's ability to fall in love with me

3. Margins

There was a reminder of this horrid feeling, The reminder that my awful life was given meaning. Saving the world, helping my lover save the world.

"Lover" is vague, we were more like, something less more possessive, but

something more doomed. We are sinking starships.

the son of hunt defined us as the most illogical aspect of love. and he made sense, we were illogical. we were young, we were honing the time we had together like a lantern about to go out.

there was story, of the marine angels of our world. and that story paved the way of the archetype that was prescribed to us.

we both knew it, the story incapsulated us. It was an archetype we could not run away from. the black angel wanted to poison the sea with its avoidance.

Life is not like the oak treehouse in our school, there is no greens in this mirage of cemented city overrun with spite.

I am tired already, I always have been, starved for the hills and the sea. In a city

that's an abyss for my poetry.

While Being stranded in a forest with an Ancient Altar after marine angels soared through the sky, to the awaiting Allegory odyssey journaled by the last messiah.

"The words tense me as the skies bleed the color of the dawn-less night, I saw a deer distilled of flesh, A creature ever so equestrian that it represents the end of the world. Armageddon is at bay so i must sacrifice this hold to the womb goddess"

The thoughts fawned on me, womb goddess had never pardoned me with love.

She had never pardoned me with any grace. Why would she now? at these hills where the world changes its course like heresy?

Because thats all she's capable of making me believe. That my heresy is her strength, Because I'm a slave to her eternal eldritch wisdom. She forbids to unravel my rancid chains until the world ends. And I can't let it.

I cannot let go of Soileh, he's the only form of grace that has ever dawned on me beyond the tunes of hysteric delusions. I cannot let go, but his morals relinquish the forges of my soul.

He is the sun, And i'll set him aflame. Thats my curse. To light a match that blazes with a never ending night. The irony of the fire that engulfs the world doing through the darkness of an eternal night.

4. Marionette

And with your ring on my finger, I could envision that the curse was a
lie.
Something I convinced myself that wasn't real. My mind mustered up
unconscious chastity to avoid the confrontation that love is something
I'm
capable of.

And then my ribs filled with warmth, Your image burnt onto my chest.
If I was
the messiah, you'd have to be my god. That's the only way this love
would
ever make sense, that's the only way we'd make sense.
But most hills were just the beginning of the bargain with my god.
And there
were no angels. It was the messiah, The god, and the uncertainty of
doomsday crawling down my waist like death.
One Fine July day I found a revelation in your temple
"Your love is the casualty, Somewhere in the atlas. Your soul will tie
you both
down by either a thread or a leash. And the wreckage of the string will
cause
armageddon"
the veins of my heart knotted at the sound of the sky bleeding the
words of my
end.

Again. There were no angels, or were there?

He was there, whatever he was supposed to be. The child of the hunt, Existing for

another key to the new era of the world.

He was what I saw, He did not worship your temple. He did not take sides.

This religion was his thesis, regardless of his theism.

And his hands crocheted a bridge made of fabric.

He is here to help me through armageddon. But how could anyone help me?

Its my poison, it's my prophecy. But no. He's here to help me craft a solution to

the end of the world.

"Why would you comply the love of a child, to the fate of the universe?" was

the question that tortured us both

Suddenly, you started stepping back from our home. Like an old man sick and

tired of everything. You started to stray, it's in your blood. You're the saviour of

the world, And I am your saviour.

And you'd not believe me if I said, It's all for the sake of the world. You'd be

crazy in love with me, but my insanity is beyond your
comprehension.

And I have to Grasp, You're younger than me, exactly a year and a half.
You're a child, just like me. But I have the burden to fight the descent
of our
lives.

> *You are my altar*
> *I am your sacrifice*
> *you are my cemetery*
> *I am your hopeless eyes*

And I'll disguise myself as your inferior, so you stay longer. I want you
to stay
regardless of how much it bleeds me, the wounds on me are frail, and
the lack
of me will matter less to the world than the loss of you.
God damn it, My love for you makes me selfish.
And your love for me makes you a coward.

I let the hunter stay a marionette with strings on the both of us.
Doesn't matter
what he does, as long as he has us glued to the same space, as long as I
pretend it's not the end of the world.

But the hunter isn't strong enough to lift off what the world has tied
onto the
fates of me and Soileh

While Being stranded in a forest with an Ancient Altar after marine angels

soared through the sky, to the awaiting Allegory odyssey journaled by the last

messiah.

"The words tense me as the skies bleed the colour of the dawn-less night, I saw a deer distilled of flesh, A creature ever so equestrian that it represents the end of the world. Armageddon is at bay so I must sacrifice this hold to the

womb goddess"

The thoughts fawned on me, womb goddess had never pardoned me with

love. She had never pardoned me with any grace. Why would she now? At these hills where the world changes its course like heresy? Because that's all she's capable of making me believe. That my heresy is her strength Because I'm a slave to her eternal eldritch wisdom. She forbids me to

unravel my rancid chains until the world ends. And I can't let it.

I cannot let go of *Soileh*, he's the only form of grace that has ever dawned on

me beyond the tunes of hysteric delusions. I cannot let go, but his morals

relinquish the forges of my soul.

He is the sun, And I'll set him aflame. That's my curse. To light a match that
blazes with a never ending night. The irony of the fire that engulfs the world
doing through the darkness of an eternal night.

Disdain Town

He arrives back at the town that destroyed him and Soileh even deeper, the wounds cut deeper as the lands start to feel familiar. Does he even have enough time to grieve his false matrydom? does he have enough will to continue?

He knew he was unlovable, that his soul was not made for love and it wasn't a defect nor was he a monster. womb goddess stitched his heart to his lungs. if he stops breathing for too long his heart stops, if he dosen't work towards the cause of existence for too long then his heart stops.

Confused and crooked he thought maybe he should hunt for something more. He didn't yet know that ancient Death followed him, a relentless shadow bound to his every step. _Moherani_, the Reaper of Forgotten Souls, was not like the other deities he had encountered. She was old, older than time itself, older than even the storm that had engulfed the world.

Moherani wasn't just a bringer of death; she was its memory, the keeper of those forgotten by history, swept away in the endless cycles of creation and destruction. She walked unseen, her presence a cold breath on the back of Suraci's neck, her footsteps silent as she trailed him through the lands. He was blind to her for now, consumed by the weight of his own guilt, but her gaze never left him. She was patient, knowing that all souls, even those of failed saviours, must eventually face her.

To look upon Moherani was to face the inevitability of endings. She was not grotesque or fearsome in the way mortals imagined Death to be. She was the reality, she was the oldest harlot of the East, her face veiled like a mourner at a funeral. She didn't carry a weapon, for she needed none. Her presence alone was enough to sever the thread of life. But for Suraci, she waited. She knew his time was not yet, though it was coming. He was marked by her, a man walking in borrowed time, and Moherani never forgot those she claimed.

As he moved through the storm-battered lands, searching for redemption, Moherani watched silently, knowing that no matter how far he wandered, he could not escape her. She was not his enemy, nor his saviour. She was simply inevitable.

5. Ancient evil

This town is poisoned by the roots of an ancient evil, and we are poisoned by
the ancient trope of burial.
I could not handle you, and you could not understand me, its easier to accept
the flaw than to work on it, its easier, to let your lover be a pyre of flames than
to find an excuse to let them live.

They would stake me up, and they would row the ground with overgrown
bales, they would pin my arms above my head to the wooden pillar, they
would engrave their horrid languages to the bottom of the pillar,
and you'd light the fire, You'd burn me away, you'd watch me die. with one
a single tear in your eyes.
You'd burn the person who loves you most, so you
could live in disdain town.

You'd live in disdain Or disgrace. In this city, there are only two options,
there are only two choices, there are two torments.

One is to be with me, One is to be in love

One is to be with them, One is to sacrifice Us.

6. Fingertips

holding your hand in silence, our fingertips crawled towards each other gushing out like winds that forbid the force of love. you reached for me, through the cracks of the pine walls.

It was raining, we danced through the severe June songs without knowing each other at all. a path of fate that we swindled across like the string of the illicit war.

And your hand has lost sight of me, I wish you did too. the shallow quest of figuring out why the world lets me down, holding a will against my humanity.

It's on repeat, the same destiny of disappointment, the same destiny of disaster.

And i'll be fine with the soot covering my body as i take the pledge to survive through this land massacred by the hoax of love.

7. Demolish

you demolished the temple I prayed for you in, you could've just taken away my tongue, but you took away my goddess. And it took you one silence to be quiet forever, yet you choose to shatter when my name is in someone else's favour.

you worship stoicism like an idol not a philosophy, your temple in a slammer, your mind is mediocrity.

and I witness you dragging yourself across the walls you nailed to avoid my scent, but what you thought never existed was just clandestine to yourself.

and i'll rebuild my temple as your mural, i'll return to my goddess, i'll find the haste of my romance, and i'll do it all over again. but i will not pray for a heretic, not for a kafir.

8. cycle

You now cycle yourself home
walk along the marble floor
you seep onto my misery bone
like a bullet's stone
Its that time again
the same hills
the same game
the heavily formidable insane
and i have it all now
a chance, fate
fear, stow
but what's stopping me now?
you adjust your angle to be in my glance
its like the universes ultimate plan
Another way of letting myself go to hell
I Don't want to think of your name
gosh my poetry sucks now
not enough metaphors left
the way you've left me without my tongue
has me hellbent

9. Hoard

i hoard your memories like the pile of unwashed clothes begging to be taken out to Laundry,
i guess the tears that swallowed your fabric did not mean anything to you,
after all how can any of my metaphors be seen replacing the blood of the sun star,
how can my metaphor not mimic your scar at your heart,
how would i get anything more than the basket of clothes washed in the sea,
maybe the lilac is from the never ending purple of our matching Tee,
Doomed to be an archetype, Waiting for fate
to weave us bright light,
but the dark of the Golden heart will always keep us uptight.

10. Cinema

the cinema of romance has your name stuck on its screen, like a cassette repeating that one unnamed Cavetown song. thinking about you is a grey line between whats love and lost, i hate to think that i loved you, pretending i can console those feelings into this little music box named "love". I know you wouldn't love be the same, its the acceptance game. and you deny your love like an enamel pin waiting to poison you every time someone asks my name. We had the same best friends, my love labelled as not true. what an english thing to do, leave me spiralling in your lilac blue. the sky is orange, even in black i can find hues of you, close my eyes to see the curls worth a fortune. i gave you green, i gave you lilac, i gave you orange, i gave you all of my favourite shades. and you left me in the dark, stuck in an one sided lovers gaze. "it was a phase" you'll say when you're old, knowing my heart was solid gold, knowing my eyes still feel like home, knowing the lilac sea never reached its western coast.

11. Kingdom

The kingdom of betrayal has your heartbeat as its anthem, you still tastle illicit on my skin, forbidden to my eyes. my iris are chained to avoid your glances, we wont see each other for a month or more. You'll look at me with the abstinence of what we could've been, I'll bury myself alive trusting that. Today a lover asked his birthday and i remembered yours, why am i cursed to your fate evermore. i have a life too, more than what your cotton eyes and jute skin sews. i'm in the absence of words to describe the lack of joy that detachment causes, but i'll feel it all. envy, fear, caged freedom, because you're just fifteen, and i am just sixteen, but seventeen this month. do you remember my birthday? have you etched it down the road to my neighbourhood? Do you miss the day we met? fearing sleep because the tent howled with the lack of settlement. and yet you denied to settle within my heart. its okay, you're forgiven. I'm the poet, i'll eat away the pain. Its my nurture, its my nature, its what i devour to survive, ***but sometimes even survival feels empty by your lack. And the sea of sorrows has got its lilac back.***

12. Dreams

your dreams have become a signature
that your love was as systematically avoided
as your fluency in the french language
somehow somewhere my first response
to the fact that you're living your best lite
makes me proud of you, unfathomably proud
We were bettas stuck in a tank of despair
with chains on our fins only one of us could see
but that was okay,
you'd never loved someone in the same pond
it was always the birds you had your eyes set on
and im going to 17 next month, and not move on
because you'll not be there to tell me happy birthday
you'll not stand in line to give me something
and maybe you still have my keychain
one with the blue and gold ancient frame
i chose it because it reminded me of you
lilac sea after all, the floor was stood

13. Songbird

I'm a silenced songbird
singing symphonies
surrendering soliloquies
to the savaged shamans of shame
They taxidermy my toxicity
Tangle up my tapestry
Teach me The Turmoil it took
To become The Tale of Tainted Taboo
nest on my negligence
null my neediness
marry my mistakes
mow on my maddening machinery
To become this falsely accused prodigy
living on the staple of instability
crafting past the azure of insanity
waiting for some divine clarity

14. Existential

I want to be pretty enough for you,
but you don't exist.
so i scar my hair off my head
i sink into the burning pyre
of what we were supposed to be.
I change and I change
to figure out who i am
and i end up becoming
more and more of your problem
and i beg for forgiveness
and i grieve my mistakes
and i buy new glasses
and have the same esoteric face
no matter how much i change
i'm only pretty for the golden hour
where your hair and my eyes
had the same shade of colour
and i become your shadow
and you become my destiny
and i wake up everyday by the remorse
of your existential epiphany

15. Wallet

I carried a picture of you in my wallet

But we went to the hills and saw ballet

this time there was no one to get drunk with

no woman to figure out our love with

The rum ran down the streets of our hometown

Where we see each other every second sundown

The evergreen season died overtime i went down

to the festive lane of your society's downtown

The secrets spilled down the hallway

Looking at each other like we're in broadway

The affair wasn't even real to me

How could I tell someone to see what i don't see

No sign of being drunk

yet talking nonsense like a heretic to a godless nun

And the world is a grave of our tragedy

and the grave worshippers call it gluttony

To drink the night

Without feeding the moon

tipsy on the stars

running into headlights by the lack of your swoon

16. Reality

I don't think love is real

then why do I look for you at every corner at the city street?

I go to the Town-mall and expect you to be there

just because you live in the apartment in front of here

just because your society lies in the midways

Of the mall, And me.

Why do i expect you to be all I see?

at every nook and cranny there is something of that makes sense only

to me

And i look back in the distance

Expecting a Silhouette of you

Expecting a Painting of you

Expecting a Mirror

But i can never find you

You're never there

but you're still everywhere

17. Scent

The sky is your scent
Is it all just pretty petty pretend?
When I'm close to you
it feels I'm closer to death
The chains on my fingertips
growing moss in my nails
I let them grow
because i was envious of your mind's jail
And I'm still sorry
I don't want you back
I'm happy my best friend is now yours
I'm happy that my heart is now yours (to fold)
And you have origami
As a subject for my heart
And I look at you living
While i boil in the survival of our past
My poetry has gotten rough
Unfamiliar, Dead, monotonous
But i cant put you into words, sunrise
as your sight I'm as clear as dust

18. Escargot

you make my escargot skin burn, the saline solution of my iris makes for the perfect seasoning on cut open wounds.

I will season the beef i'm not allowed to eat, cook it, burn it, get the curse of another mother and wash it down my throat like a daily chore.

Do you understand how horrible the lack of you is? how desperate my heart is? for a sign that you'll return?

it's like my withering house has a back door you sneak you in incase you arrive next decade into your senses that your love was unnoticed by you.

but till then, i'll be served up in your platter and you'd be disgusted. But until you try anything more than a pumpkin pie, you wont be satisfied.

19. My young

whenever i think im in love it feels like im chasing a fox in the shadows of my curtains that blocks the black walls of my bedroom,

I feel the grave being starved of me, even death can't make me hers. I just want to be someone to someone permanently. You took that away from me.

So i'm trying to find a fire that burns beyond my tendencies to be miserable. I want to be buried into the wind through flames.

There is no salt lake city, none we can go to. we cannot go to the moon to cascade our love, we will never not be illicit. and you'll never be someone who loved me enough to fight.

So let me die, un-curse me from immortality. please. i beg you.
because i dont think i genuinely am capable of love that doesn't take roots in warcraft

And this town reeked off of our end, it howled like hyenas on the edge of the fallen concrete. And i could not help but discover a grimoire that's not mine. The final gift of a book that reveals the secrets of the end of the world.

It listed the promise of the curse bearer. and the workings of the entities that have casted their fragile fortunes upon me,

And I think i started speaking in curses, trying to fondle the force of nature that etched you out of my chest. I could blame the entire world and not you. Why not? just because you were young? or because i envisioned you as my young?

Did I want to raise you up like a child, stitch up your wounds with the flavour of lime, what did i want?

20. Dinner

I ate my empathy for dinner, and the goddess became distant. I was a
starving child, chewing off blades of honour and early remorse.

My lips scared with the metal of the sword that gritted my teeth silver
white, and they looked at me with disgust in their eyes.

I wore the wool of war westside, and the scars cover my dawning eyes.
I only see faults, I only see lies.

Who do you trust when your goddess is not on your side? waging wars
against not having ample of time? becoming the marauder of your own
throne? the slave of your own shine?

But I still eat it, the empathy. I'll chug it down with revenge like its
irish cream, i'll drink the whiskey with coffee just because it's neat.

I want you to know, you made me a cannibal, you made me a thief.

21. May she Drape the Sea

she'd drape the sea on her like a garment

wear all your warmth

she would sink on the viscosity

that you and I had lost

She'd wear all the purples,

Lilacs, Violets and maybe Greens

she looks like porcelain

And yet she's scared of the screen

The tiredness is sturdy,

Fate is consistently weaved

the way you're past it all

and its just me who feels this misery

I'm obsessed with drawing fishes

and my veins gush out the dirty ocean

and its ironic how she drapes it on

and you don't even want to admit the commotion.

then i made you plough the field

grow a land savaged by your poison tea

when you didn't believe in me

And i lost the heart that you locked with the key

But you dont see the drapes yet

you dont envision enough death

For I travel too you too

hunt you through

lose the stiches he sew

Rage lake

In the gist of figuring out his reality, he finds himself on the way to Agandeviyan, The eternal fire. The one that swallowed the Nile and Ganges, devoured the afterlife and the path towards it. As long as you stayed in their grace you were immortal. The covenant of dawn was their making.

"The Covenant of Dawn is a religious group deeply devoted to Agandeviyan, worshipping them as a beacon of light in an otherwise eternal night. The Covenant believes that while a god exists, that god—referred to as the Womb Goddess—is cruel and horrible, trapping the world in endless darkness. The members, mostly women who have lost their lovers, hold a doctrine that this eternal night is a punishment, and they must despise the Womb Goddess until the dawn finally arrives.

Agandeviyan, however, is seen as their source of hope, the light that could one day end this perpetual night. The nuns within the Covenant are warriors, hunting down pests that plague the land. As a boon from Agandeviyan, their memories are erased, offering them a strange form of solace through forgetfulness and freeing them from the pain of their past lives. The Covenant's mission and beliefs represent a tension between faith, bitterness, and hope.

The covenant may provide solace to a godless child, The covenant may house and humour this naked "boy" but it will never home him, for his home is his devotion to those who abandoned him.

Suraci needs to validate his dissonance, the rage and love that tumbles down his skin needs to be proven, needs to be shared. Someone will have to empathise, or at least sympathise. someone would know how it feels to be abandoned by your mother and your lover,

someone must... right?

22. Tailorbird

I utter your name twice
in silence, in sync with my tears
you are not mine anymore
not for almost an year
and the tailorbird in my garden sews together leaves and i watch her
from afar like a patient in line waiting to get stitches on my torn apart
heart

23. Flock

you flock the crows towards my demise. feed off the remaining scarcity of you, scabbing your left wounds, as my rotting flesh burns by the beaks of the cunning birds. I wonder if this is all you are, a murder of crows, and the death of me.

24. Curfew

my fingers have a curfew on holding the pen
it's not new to me,
that my mind is an aristocracy
I'll let my arms wrap around my resignation, It's a vintage piece of an
olden letter because I can travel through the city And still not make
my book look pretty
you'd say it's defiance
it's a lack of my compliance but it's the lit-up candle of mine that's
been burning for years
The candle with wax
Basking in the shade of my loss

25. Do gods visit cemeteries?

Do gods visit cemeteries?

Isn't that what you left of the temple we built?

Is the intoxication of immortality, stronger than my epiphany?

You were the god of my temple now I am the god of your grave

26. Prophet

You call me a prophet
so I feed you the revelations You listen to longing
And you stake me up at the whim
And you ask me the truth
and I write it up on fresh flesh
and tie it to the pigeon's neck
to send it over to your window seethe
I am the concoction you drink
made from the carcass of the man diary
I'm the one who gallows down your throat treating your insides like
my society
I am your sickness I am your exile
I am your finding
I am your reconciling
I build you up
and I hold you tightly I'm the loose string
and I'm the almighty
You can burn me as a witch You can gurn on my face
but you'll yearn at my demise Because I'm your entirety

   Suraci's ego has started to feed onto Soileh's demise. To blame an
innocent you ruined, It's a testimony to your authenticity. Soileh was
a child with the world in his hands. and you were just a slave made to
not even serve him, to love him. And you failed. Your prophecy
devours you suraci, Your death awaits you.

27. Free me

• 42 •

Will all this rage in me, ever free me? when the heat of my angst burns down my cage, does it burn down my home too? I don't want to be a wild child with a blade of fire running across the dry fields causing arson. Then why do I? All this rage was once silence, all this silence was bleeding wounds, and all the wounds were my nature. I want to be silent without being silenced, I want to be a child without arson. I want to be heard and told that my love overshadows my lack.

But it just never does. And I stay in the incompetence of my work. A scared child heals his wounds with fire that burns others. my blaze cannot escape me without harming you. why is this curse so everlasting? whom does this rage conquer? when it burns down my home, the one place I'm supposed to belong

28. Bathe in Blasphemy

I bathe in blasphemy

In a town of your Hatred

In the workings of everything you decline how dare you curse me with this?

How dare you show my rebellion as insanity How dare you dehumanize my fate

How dare you make a citadel of bone And blame me for your harvest

If your divine is so omnipotent why do you need my sacrifice why do you need my history why do you need me as the price

I cant be your martyr

I cant be another religion I cant be another War Again.

Your town is my home and my home is your ruin leave me alone,

Or guide me through.

29. June of '23

Somewhere in the haze of memories...
We danced around the campfire on June of '23
and I burnt my finger when you gave me the ring
and you've become the blaze grazing the love out of my spine
burning the matchstick on time leaving our sanity behind
Again and again,
buried into the ground
with the silver chains
on your neck and my knee on your chest
Do you like it forbidden
eat it alive now
my flesh is dinner
and your denial is my vow
soothe my forsaken soul
for the sorry of your false guilt
and the hound of your honour morgue
waiting to devour
our last closure riled cloth made of solid gold

30. Intuitions

I cannot keep swearing at the sky, keep screaming at the ghost of you. the poltergeists are tired of my words and your ears are just under the same moon as me, yet in disbelief of my faith.

The gods never help, the birds of paradise are in paradise, and we have our wings snipped in this hellscape of a city. The same angels that vow to keep us safe rain the horror of blindness upon us. cursing us with indifferent intuition.

And you keep raising this high hope scar at the disposal of your own worship, every sacrifice is emotional, then what happened to lambs and goats?

I talk to you, look you in your blind eyes. Are you the epitome of the grievance's

love high? waiting in the shadows to hold me through the eternal nightmare that

you forecasted. putting the morals in a casket, my bloody clothes in your laundry basket. cleaning the evidence at a halt.

wish I wasn't your bravest soldier, begging for the war to end, just to find out you're playing pretend anytime you say love's waiting at the end. but the road less taken is my destiny, if you've crafted my path, isn't it ironic? is it so hard to give me a death where I'm a martyr and not the prey? *don't I have i say?*

31. 316

316 days, And I'm still cursedly tied to you. In my dreams, and my damned hopes. I wish to never see you, but I can't avoid wanting your glances in the roadways. I hunt for you like a staple, in the midwest of my mind. you exist in an oversaturated orange house, with an overgrown garden in the middle of nowhere. You sit on a rocking chair, reading the latest issue of my journal I wrote you before my death. you rock yourself to sleep and stay stranded awake by midnight. hoping to see my ghosts in your bedroom. But it's too late, ghosts are

invisible remember? You ought to unlearn me, orange house boy. Your overgrown hair had blinded you, my overgrown hair has been cut down to shreds. so I could see your flaws, to rest you off my mind. Bleeding through my eyes open in a storm to watch you walk through and save you. But you'd wish I

died. doesn't everyone? it's okay, I'll leave next year. and we'd stop becoming each other's phantoms. we'd stop becoming a past unwanted.

32. Shamelessly

There is the universe, shamelessly urging me to return to him. to return home. but does it make me weak or strong? to not go back?
every corner of my eyes, his silhouette watches me. holds my face in his palm and says "come back to me, come back home". every curly haired boy becomes him, every tree becomes him, every nest becomes him. every shade of brown is him, every hue of orange is him, every piece of gold is him, every round glass is him, everything that cuts me is him, everything that makes me bleed is him.
people are rivers, they flow away. thats why you need boats, or you need to bleed. so they carry a part of you with them
We lost our language in the ruins of your temple, I try to make new ones. but none of them have words for the way i loved you in.

33. Ragelust/Familiar

The covenant of dawn seems familiar to me, the Ragelust of the people and their loathsome anger for the gods and their service towards them regardless.

it reminds me how the worship of you is limited to me, and my desire to hate you, my desire to abandon you and yet I stay at your feet with rancid chains clawing through my tendons.

The covenant of dawn wants to dismantle the god it's asking back. And I feel The covenant of dawn will succeed before I do.

But that's impossible,

But everything seems more plausible than the verity of our reunion, than the risk of our bond becoming anew. I wonder if the covenant of dawn has in its scripture, a mention of you and me.

"The suraci and sunrise, are apart from the same place that bonds them together The suraci and sunrise, want the same place that disdains their feathers"

Suraci arrives at the temple of Agandeviyan

34. Misery Devourer

I keep blazing my throat with urgency to understand what it is, what you are, who I am. and why does your name cause arson in my ribs. Who are you to turn my misery into fuel for the Agandeviyan, She's already eaten my thoughts for good, she's already dispatched my prayers of you from my own selfishness. then who are you? That has such a deep causality in my roots, Who are you in the backyard of my mind waiting to devour the traces of me? Who are you? That burning the thoughts of you kills the hope in me?

You can lie to me, and I can lie to you. But I'll be the one burning, You'll be the one to fuel it. But you don't care. I don't understand. Why is my heart so filled with someone who doesn't care? It's a shame to my serpentine soul, that a mere grave with a casket holds the runes of my death.

35. Vrakisorrianna

I wrap my bones in velvet lies to keep the truth from piercing your heart. you think I worship the fire, but it is not the flames I kneel for. I heard kneeling makes me the closest to the devit. the fire won't burn me—it doesn't want to. I could step into the furnace and remain unscathed because it knows. it knows I am already ash, already hollowed out by my devotion, my desperation. the fire sees through the facade, and yet I still beg to be consumed by it, to be made part of the heat that shapes your hands.

you stand before the fire, blacksmith to your craft, forging destinies while I stand before you, praying to merge with the flames that obey you. but it's not your love I crave—no, I know better than that. I could set myself ablaze, and you would still be bound to the fire. your heart may lie with me, but your soul is destined to be with the flames. I am not asking for your love; I am asking for annihilation. let me burn, let me become part of the inferno that holds you, so that in some twisted way, i can be closer to you.

the fire is your true devotion. no matter where your heart wanders, no matter who it touches, it always returns to Agandeviyan, to the heat that binds you to your craft. and i, knowing this, still throw myself into the flames. i am not the martyr or the sinner—I am the offering. I tear at my soul, hoping to find something worthy to offer, but all I find is the same sin that keeps me tethered to this eternal plea.

you're not the god I worship; you are my priest, my executioner. I want to become the flames that wrap around your fingers, moulded by the same force that shapes you. but the fire holds back, knowing that no matter how much I beg, I will never be part of its core. I could strip away my flesh, tear open my chest, but even then, I would not be enough. I would not be purified; I would still be on the outside, a shadow cast by your devotion, lingering in the smoke.

so tell me, am I the victim of my worship, or have I simply become another one of your tools held close to the fire, but never truly consumed?

36. Agandeviyan

Agandeviyan

"Do you think your love was the reason you set yourself aflame or the belief that nothing can burn more than his idea"

Suraci

"I think the only thing that burns more than his idea is who I thought I was, I was no gentle lover trying to accompany him through the cascades of turmoil, I was a part of your flame that burnt him. He tried to touch me and I crafted wounds on his nails that I envied so very much. I have been burning him more than you can burn anyone. I am guilty in the court of courtships,
And I don't even know if this was the result of the curse or my casualty"

Agandeviyan

"you do not understand your dissonance child, the question was simple. I do not care for your faults, mortals are prone to commit immorality, the question was whether it's your love burning you or your lack thereof"

Suraci

"then why don't you let Vraakasorriana burn? why don't you let her be free

of her sins?"

Agandeviyan

"You don't burn sins you wash them away, And I killed the Ganges. I am but a god, my fire cannot be done impure by tempted temporal love"

Suraci

"yet you are not strong enough to burn the love of the one who's not tempted nor temporal, you could not burn me. so give Vraakasorriana my grace, Give her my fire and let her burn through.

Agandeviyan

all this rage won't turn to freedom for her, no one washes their sin in a sinless world so why'd I pollute myself for her grace? it doesn't matter if I can, I'm not made to must. Do you understand? being a god does not make me owe you a lack of sin, I could burn her love, I could wipe her memory, but I'd not burn her sin. for she has committed none. Until she understands her love. I cannot ash it.

37. Victim of Worship (ft. Sukriti Sinha)

I would set myself on fire if it meant I could keep you warm.

I could become the flames and you'd still be freezing.

The ice would cut through me and I would step back because I cannot let this blood stain you. I could wash off trails of my rotten carcass so my maggots don't maim you.

I would dissolve into ash and let the wind carry me far from you, so my decay doesn't cling to your skin.

I am a saint poisoning my idol, I'm a heretic cleaning my chapel.

Who are you? My god or my religion? Am I the martyr or the sinner in this twisted devotion? Regardless of my devotion, I am a victim of your worship.

I tear at my flesh, hoping to reveal a heart pure enough to worship you, but all I find are sins etched deep within my bones.

Bones black as the scathed willow tree after you struck it either the bolt of my romantic guillotine.

I would strip away whatever is left of my humanity to become the shrine you deserve, yet I fear that even then, my prayers would go unanswered, my sacrifice in vain.

You're a god born in my heart's hurricane, the tempest flows like betrayal in your veins. No prayer could save me from your doomsday.

So tell me, who are you—my salvation or my damnation?

That's an answer that would give Morningstar vindication, that's a question for God's denunciation.

Burn at your altar, but the flames only illuminate my flaws, i've built this temple in your name, but the walls are crumbling, stained by the smoke of my desperation. And the sea is rising, the storm is tense, and the clouds are tired of this pretence.
Everyone watches like the stars are falling, striking your velvet orange; to become nothing more than an abandoned god who we resent.
Would wrap my bones in velvet lies to keep the truth from piercing your heart. I could tear down every idol, shatter every relic, yet I'd still be bound to you, chained by a faith I can't renounce. If you are my god, why do I feel so forsaken? And if you are my religion, why do I feel so lost? Is this love or merely obsession dressed in holy robes?
If you are my sanctuary, why do I feel so exiled? And if you are my god, why do I tremble in fear, as though I'm unworthy of your grace?

38. Last Summer

The sky is the same summer shade all over again,

the warms, the breeze, the ever so glistening drizzle that makes city

petrichor smell like you.

But city petrichor is a sham,

your smell can only be traced back to the mountains, the hills where

we met. where solitude met at first glance syphoning.

Japanese became a part of us,

the moon was pretty, you shined like the stars we both had the same

vision in our eyes

only one wanted to accept it.

"Koi No Yokan" is the feeling of seeing the potential of falling in love,

I don't know what happened that day, what made me the way that was,

What made you so blinded to stray away.

It was June, then it was October. Now it's March. Six months as if

nothing happened, as If you didn't see all of me, as if we didn't know

what was going to happen.

We prophesied a doom, and the destiny was for you to hate me. You

would never call me your best friend. Would you?

Bleach the sun the shade of my skin I hid my ribs within the pine trees

Thorough out the caverns of your house

For I want to find the cavity of the Sea's

The songs are sung in the echos of colossal sounds like a mysterious

symphony

where my heart is covered in bruises of you and my bones are covered

in leaves

The vines grow through the promise

the prophecy has its incense lit You know the way destiny works you

know we are doomed to meet

I'll survive the storm for a week

so I can save you from solemn Sovereignty It is the best of both worlds

all over again trying to not sacrifice myself on your merit

I'll have to face you tomorrow

like it doesn't make me taste the rain

because it's doomsday on Monday

and you didn't stay.

we talked it out

October 7, Bleeding out you wear the tempest gown

and I'll bury myself in your hometown

and it's storming back now I can see your house

the naked buildings writing "Gaur"

the taste of you is so sour.

I go through a valley of your residence

and I can smell Petrichor because it sounds like your name

tolerating your absence like the ambrosia for pain

and yet you've maimed my heart like a white and withered blood stain

The war starts again tomorrow.

I watch your memories like a child with Quilt Then why does the

image of us together make me feel the existence's guilt

You walked in front of me

with a speckle of the haunted scene and the radio played on repeat

"it's school vacation, Again, take your seat"

it's all destiny

and it will only mess with me

and and the end you'll spoil the rug

magenta, with blood scarlet clean

And I'll dream of the day

you'll not drain me out in the clouds

with walls for your kingdoms and lesser angels throughout

Its alchemy

The way you mould our forbidden chemistry The way it's all illicit like

a movie scene

The way it makes me wonder "Who is he?"

and you like her too same mind, same tone

looking at the pomegranate evermore

knowing I'd trade her for your soul

the blade of you is bitter my scars are succulent green

I knew you worshipped venom I knew you hated me

And I loved you through the Venice alleys I loved you through the

Chail forests

I missed you through the cycle byline I wished for you to my vicious

fates.

and yet the colours dry out the desert

where I lost my hourglass made from only sand And yet the purples

stain my scar

like it is a tattoo carved onto my hand

The world is ending and you did not come over so I talk to your

tombstone dialling your number by carving them onto the soil of your

bones. But it rings to nowhere, the landline does not connect to hell.

The strings don't shrivel down destiny. Now the world has ended, 11

months and 1 day. Does it mean

something? Has it ever meant anything? to anyone but me? It's the

apocalypse, And I'm thinking and thinking. But I am too young to

think. Too young to figure out why others are horrible. And you burn up my skin, you dissociate my scars.

You're not even real, not anymore. So I will listen to Mitski because the Cavetown

record is broken. And every inch of love was scattered and unspoken. Or it didn't

exist at all. I can't figure it out, Being an experiment rather than an experience never lasts. So I'll smoke a fake cigarette, and pretend Grape juice is wine.

Become addict to nihilism, and marry off a random girl as my wife. I'll write poems in the morning, about how death is the biggest gift. I'll burn down Sylvia's fig tree. And anchor down a Battleship's stained cemetery.

You weren't always wretched, you cracked a smile through the hollows ever so often, signing your stay within the rules of my warmth. But you're a vile muse, a foolish lover and a flawed liar. So i'll let you go, watch you drown in the ocean i sailed you through hours with.

i have cut down the poison through the shards of the mirror where i set my hair everyday. the distortion of our tale was only temporary for your sake.

the white in my hair flared like the wiseness that lacked in the sparkle of your eyes. watching you watch my demise.

you are just young and naive and unwilling to change your destiny, and I beat the gravel up until it cleanses all the misery.

I bathe in the lake wounded where you wash your clothes, and I'm bleeding out

yet your biggest concern is the blood on your clothes.

Repugnant Ruins

The Rage calmed down, Suraci gulped down the anger and witnessed a surreal sense of calm, but he was not satisfied. He was wronged by the three layers of the world that held up his stature.

His Devotion towards his Goddess,

His Love towards his best mate

His Trust towards humanity.

That's all he had to hold himself accountable, all he had to save the world. His side of the bargain was to be loved. But his soul wasn't made to be loved, He was the embodiment of the Messiah.

Suraci was never loved, never understood. Fated to fathom the insensitivity towards the world and to the world he was a normal human, to the world he was a child making stories. But Suraci witnessed the cruelty of it all.

His life was established on servitude and war, He was built upon and for silent destruction, to wear an invisible crown that gives him powers no one could see, he was an unseen king among men but he was not God enough to prove it.

But that made him a slave. And a slave can't be anything but a person filled with unwanted servitude

With shackles made of knives that if he tried to break, would cut his veins.

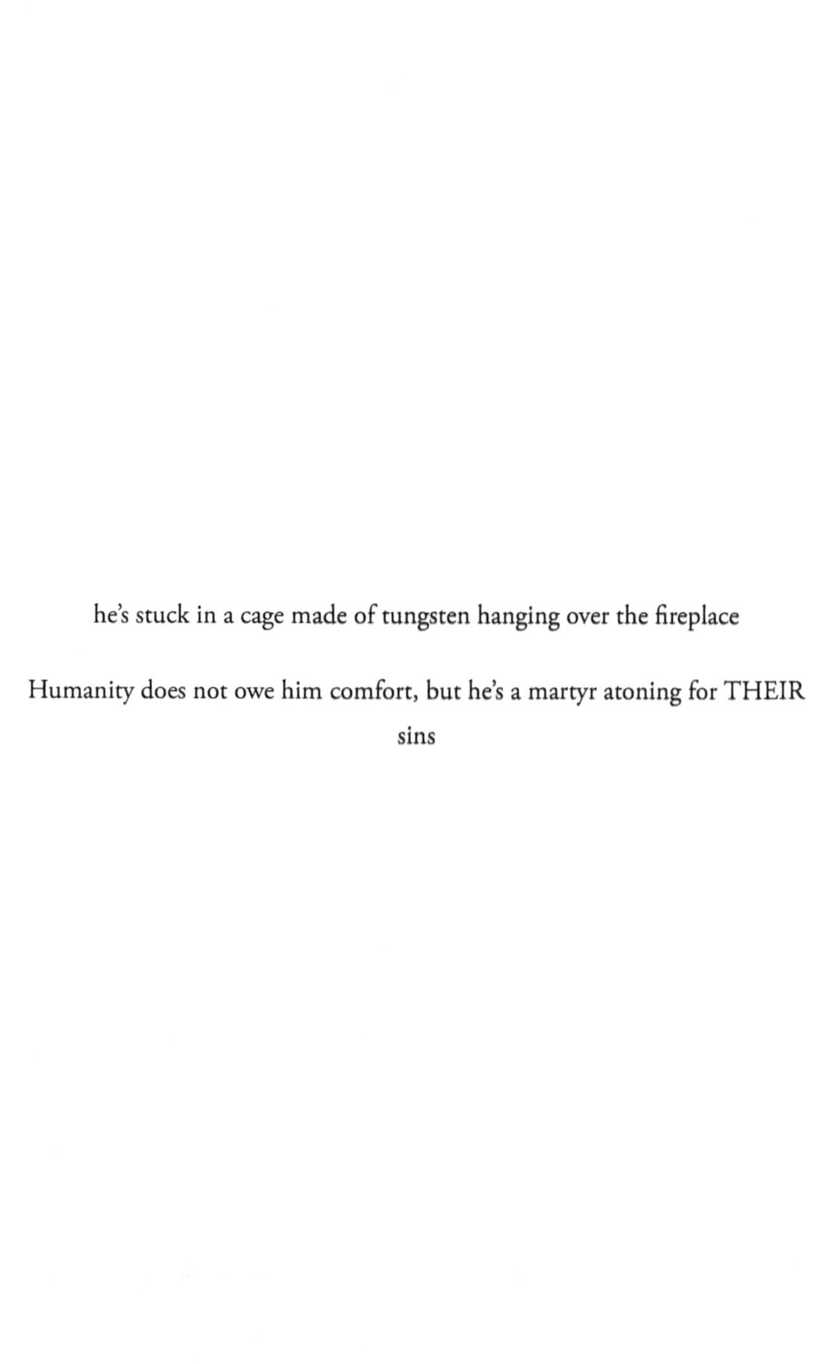

he's stuck in a cage made of tungsten hanging over the fireplace

Humanity does not owe him comfort, but he's a martyr atoning for THEIR

sins

Suraci's rage had watered down, with not much hate but a lot of questions, he travels through to the Lilac sea. Since the Ganges was devoured, the Lilac Sea was where the ashes of the dead were submerged, it was the place Soileh must've been or his absence at least.

This was also the place he dreamed about all the time, the sea where he was drowning and Soileh stood shoulder up with fierce flames in his eyes that felt like a divorce, the realization that in a world where Soileh's silent and watching Suraci as he drowns. He feels no guilt, no sadness, not an ounce of disruption by the forever lack of his best mate.

But the goal was to find the Lilac Lady, The lady who knows the most about Womb Goddess. He had to get there. I had to get there.

39. Flocking

And the crow stopped flocking above my house every morning, The
song of you was forgotten by it,
And then as the song was swallowed down the throat of the crows, so
was the sun, you fed my mornings to a mourning bird.
I needed the warmth, I needed you.

40. Chapel

flushed your chapel

down the flood of the lilac sea,

The storms begged to devour the inscriptions on the pillar,

the gods wanted our tragedy written onto Olympus cathedrals.

And I left you biting the flood

and left you drowning enough

let the gods believe my loyalty

how fate is my casualty

But I begged Gulliver.

And got you a ticket to my pocket

and the picture of you

in the tin altar, you should've guessed.

Your betrayal was not enough for me to let the gods not suffer

The heartache was not enough for me to envision myself as nothing

but Lucifer

I said I'd poison god for you

Sham is not even a scratch onto the pillar.

41. Apology To Achilles

And In this awe of his lack, I could see colours that haven't existed for millennia,

The scarlet of Aphrodite The cloud of Athena

The constitution of Hera

And the Rage Of Achilles

No hero was happy Achilles, You were right.

The sense of love always beguiles the tunic of gods. The itch of immortality always leaves scars.

But I didn't want to be a hero Achilles. heroes win wars.

No Achilles, You don't understand, I AM the war, I am the pedestal of bloodshed, I

am the mosaic of a million deaths, I am the messiah of armageddon.

I was never the saviour, Achilles

I was the ceramic sword of Artemis

I was the Storm, all along

I bled the bleeding of billions, Achilles

42. Hoard

saw your head hoarding the thoughts of me along with the gold of the gods that light as your love for me.

The bellflowers danced on your temple like the school oak house's canopy.

Where you sat beneath with me on the grounds of our last memory.

I remember the turmeric remedy when you broke your ankle, and the way you

would've swallowed poison for me.

You were the wisteria growing on me, snapping onto my bones like it's your

home. And I wanted to be that. Your home.

You were the thunder that blazed the soul of mine, rearranged my heart like it was a marionette of your chemistry, and you became a part of my tapestry

and you have always just been ever so pretty. envisioning the breath that gave

life to Persephone, Bringing me winter every October you're away from me.

43. Pay heed

And if Achilles saw me, would he pay heed to my misery? tell me how nothing feeds Tartarus more than a saviour of vague bold promises? Would he see how I love and lose and discredit the existence of that romance on the brink of a new

life? Loving and dying, slaughter and sacrifice, A war no one else can see, so no one can star in. A battle that no sun, no moon, only the ones in the stars can see?

Would Achilles slip me down a bottle of his favourite wine, just so i get through this with a mind intoxicated with something weaker than lost love's misery? or would he break the bottle down my spine and tell me to heal the wounds that are visible?

Would Achilles sympathise, seeing his devotee kneel to his fate, and become another manuscript to be altered and loved once existence breaks its breath for me?

Would Achilles come down? for me? to fix the prophecy he was the victim of?

44. Sinless

You were my homeland and you were stolen

by the absence of our words

now I'm exiled

to my own heart

one that's been decaying

you sacrificed me and outcasted me to your hell so you could be god

now the chains of my ankle burn me more

with every sight of yours

the spear is still through my chest your betrayal still stings like a curse But

I still worship you.

As if you'll come back one day

lay your immortal feet near my slammer hold me in your arms, let me die

sinless. **please.**

45. Fifteen

Fifteen is such a peculiar age to be, the wiseness beyond your years sinks up your rigid bones and makes you see the world like a mirage of sinful hope. The greatest time to be alive, to feel it all to the content that you melt into the earth with your stubbornness. At fifteen the world seems all too much, all too boring yet all too exhausting. It becomes a stride of strange moments, your love becomes frail and you latch onto the edge of someone trying to make it through. You feel you're too wise, you want wiser. No other fifteen-year-old would suffice, so you beg poets to paint and become a cardigan resting under the weight of your fate. You try to strike a slit down your palm but you're no Alexander. you're just fifteen. the sky turns red and you're fifteen and it is the end of the world but you will not agree your love meant enough. because it's wise for you to sacrifice yourself so they don't crucify themselves. Your love is stronger than your discreet martyrdom.

The world is cruel, and you are just fifteen.

46. Biting The knife

The cursed child won't fall in love tonight He is too busy biting the rusted knife that he was honing for the last three times he was shown that espionage is for the guilty
the wiseness of the borrowed rabbit escaping the deer's gaze
a hungry herbivore is more vulgar than the starving feline in mane
And the vile vicinity between me and your hauntings hanging myself
up on the trail to your wanting
My mean eyes and your missed plot-lines
and my lack of self-control from figuring out your fated signs
And you watch me watch you
like so many lovers do
only to be true
when the door has been tinted our hue
Because the cursed child is me
And you're the curse wrecking through the lilac sea on a storm that's
literally the only vocality screaming for you to swim against me.

47. The ghost of you

And the ghost of you cusps my face in its frozen hand, finding comfort in the graveyard of your silence. And all the words lost to your enlightenment to be a portrait of somebody else.

And there is no cure, Never has been one. there has been no way love can be mended, just because it slits you up, leaves scars on your back, just because it makes you bleed. doesn't make it a sword. welding love does not make you a

warrior, gripping on hope doesn't make you a soldier, and being the most

insatiable experience does not make you a blacksmith.

And the ghost of you lives on the oakwood tree of the school, I sit under it and i think of the phantoms we knew. All the little moments where I was within the concept of you. All the times you didn't want to understand the wounds you couldn't sew.

You could just be another person, who listens to me like I'm a story. Like you

wish for me in the incandescent glory. And you're still the most beautiful thing in

the sight of mine, hating you is my most irrational lie. because you're the

prophecy, and I'm the sword that beheads everything to do with our destined life.

48. Sometimes

I still feel you sometimes through my chest sometimes, the spear is still
in it.
I can feel how you felt, your company, my misery.
I can feel you,
It is like nostalgia but worse because it's not a memory
it's just a sense of you with me.
And it's been a year almost
and I look at your grave
and ask myself why are you sleeping its 4:38 PM
come back to life sunrise
make the world feel less like a puzzle again full-fill our prophecy of
sunrise
let us be more than people who were maimed

49. Surgeon

Your hair was rough and sun-dusted, Sparkling hints of oranges and hues of starlight. I swarm my fingers through your curls, I touched the sun and survived. Your skin was laden with sin, with desire. It reddened to my touch. And the sharpness of your jaw cut through my sight, your lips trembled like clouds before rain and your earthen skin had this purity of clay to it. this sensation of being ever so mouldable. Your neck was tensed, and Your chest was scarred.

I didn't tell you, but your scar made me cry. it cut through your chest. It had tampered with your heart. Only I should've touched your heart, The jealousy of a surgery was incomprehensible to me. A betrayal that occurred before my conscience was freckled.

And you were freckled, with genuine smile and admiration. I sit at your grave. And beg you to crawl back to me. You can still choose to live, It's just me now. You promised that when the world would end, you'd stay by my side, And you betrayed me.

You, The surgeon, God. Everyone Betrayed me.

50. Windshield

The windshield was broken by you in my nightmare
then the next day you're all I see
even though you were gone for basketball
I see you through the rusted staircase of this school's hall
I sat on your last June seat accidentally
Another June over and you're still the same controversy
bleeding through my deck of memory
Burying your references In my subconscious for you to hold my hand
in this painfully desired dream
And for old time's sake,
Will you hang out with me during the lunch break? And skip your
lunch so we could go for a walk? Or was i someone with too much
talk?
August And The rusted Staircase hold Then why do I remember you
so well
watching movies in '23 about things that are just enough about us
Because it's never you and me, in any universe.

51. Her Grief

I felt your mother's grief on my ribs the way she looked at me at smiled
expecting me to tell her hi
but both you and her make a bittersweet goodbye
I cripple at the tones of your skin the curls of your hair
the need of your whim
and the lack of the lack of your stares
You dwindle on me
like a hurricane to a hill seaming like nothing can hurt
pretending your stomach doesn't have a mill
And you walk me through the west like your mother's unrest
why did we share the same death of the same sun, of the same nun
so devout to be profound in the art of autumn

52. Thoughts

This misery's so embedded in my existence that waves must wage wars to decide who gets to wash off my sins

and the pathetic thing is, that the waves originate from the ocean of desolate myths. not the redemption you think they'll bring

I had begged God to let me be a child, but maybe because she's immortal she doesn't understand age. Or maybe my voice is faint enough to get lost in the wishes I have halted

The western winds suspend my legacy

I battle the hurricanes in your name and it's just the vulgarity that hurts me-

The winds shift, and Suraci's nostalgia halts.

He's at the tower, The Lighthouse.

And someone Awaits him...

53. Moherani (Sara Shah)

bride of doom. mother of woe.

my neck homes garlands stolen off mourners, strung together with the whisper of their final breaths.
dare you to forget
that though you grew to kiss the winds you are rooted to the same soil.
you can caress the soft underbelly of the sparrows.
forget your violence and pretend you had always been kind pretend,
on some strange plane you are entitled to peace and the gentlest of men. My feet are cursed,
my feet prophesies wastelands. the very earth will crumble
and swallow whole, what refuses to kneel.

and what breaks you, suraci?

this perverse adamance you wield, how mulishly, your eyes reject the light. some nights I wake up strangely craving to be your slaughterhouse to dust your hair with arsenic and drown your journals in kerosene, till every poem you wrote runs down the pages and drips onto my palms.
some nights I stir longing to taste the saline pooling in your eyes
to sink my hands in your mangled chest till your dreams soak my nail beds.

<u>*but what makes you, suraci?*</u>

I cannot recall the exhaustion of Chase yet I heave? your catalogued guilt, grief binds into the heaviest of pages and I cannot touch them without flinching. the cold of your air feathers with disdain. scorching. the end claims all, I believed. I claim all but paradox.
and what is a man when your blood has stilled? are you not just a carcass? and what is death when death cannot hold?
your regret denies you repentance. your love, transcends it.

54. Death Talks to me

Death talks to me like I'm her best friend like she can replace the girl who I have promised Boston like she can replace the boy who lives in Lucknow like she can replace the girl who draws with her soul like she can replace the boy who talks like he's an old soul. Like she can replace that one lover as if he isn't the only person who could make sense of me.

Death is my oldest companion, one that has haunted me since I was seven, telling

the star I'll join them through the mortuary for all the love rests.

I used to think as a child that death turns people into stars, that constellations are incomplete because there are people yet to be counted in. and oh how badly did it burn to find the sun is a star, that when I die I won't be the one who's the brightest mark.

And yet. The constellations will forever stay empty, the sky will forever weep,

and stars will be a metaphor, and death my companion.

And how I weep to rot, how I bleed to not.

How I exist, to be in death's caught.

Moherani and Suraci agreed, over their want for his death,
A bride married to murder and her suicidal son
And both have this saddening grief of Suraci's Immortality
But for the first time,

This Death could see herself through the lack of light in
Suraci's eyes

55. Lady Lilac (Priti Jha)

My home lies in the amber of light that once illuminated what lies beyond the eye's reach, **beyond the veil of life.**

My sea of scornful depth speaks to me. The hunger of the dead, greed of the alive and fate of those stuck in between is for me to devour. Or glorify.

now in the dusk's wake your presence demands of me what I lost long ago. oh suraci, how bitter and naïve. you ask of me a question in a language I am no longer fluent in, you ask of me the why and how of it all, oblivious to the empathy you're drenched in. The womb goddess abandoned both of us.

does she still speaks of me as if I'm the vermilion of fire she burns her palms in,

just to feel close to me? But destiny pities no god. To be a witness as the flames of arson consume the grandeur of our love; my lighthouse now homes the ashes of our tangled fates-bound to collide but never intertwine-instead of the sense of direction.

You ask of a path but your eyes refuse to follow mine. draped in your linen of forsaken sanity, you carry your angst on sleeves. But what use is it of, when you're cursed to be lost just as my waves are, in the vast blues. **When you're fated to kiss the wind that refuses to carry you away,** just so the longing ignites and swallows your reluctance to be the pathetic hero of a tragic tale.

To let go of resentment is the answer to your cruelty. Looking for a way out in this labyrinth of abyss, you are no god. look for a path that leads you to liberation, look for the apology apostle, for redemption is the only certainty.

Lady Lilac showed Suraci Seabed Cellar, The cellar within the depths of the lighthouse. but the narrator's conscience gets disrupted talking about it. There is a curse on this narrative, one that must be unravelled.

56. Pray to the Sea

the oceans have come for me, to take me away, i pray to the Sea to let me stay, to make a promise that love's on its way, but the ocean salt rubs on my wounds, and the scars bleed the ocean pink, i wait for you to sail me away in a home ship.

I wonder if you'd run to the ocean with me, take me away like a hawk with its prey, kiss me in the sea of says, to make sure that the world ends and we still find a way.

I'll figure you the great pirate's treasure, I'll give you scars that you put on necks, I'll give you hands to hold around the neck, I'll give you palms that promise the way.

And I'd make you a map of me, in case I'm taken, in case my mind is mistaken, in case you don't feel like fighting Kraken.

57. Last winter

your eyes are my mortuary your words are my cemetery your sight is
history
And the longing of you is poetry
Yet you're here for everyone but me And that's just "destiny"
there is a tree in the backyard of my heart it has a sparrow nest, empty,
overgrown
the eggs rot with the time we never even had together
now they warm up to the summer heat and the way you cycle the
byline
you have so much more time but it is not for me, it is not mine
we are divorced sparrows
my wings don't work anymore and you soar up the sky like Icarus
What a regal curse
and you have the nest upon you too waiting to have a reunion on the
first of June the broken tents, the dead cocoons
saying the same words while looking at the moon
yet love is despicable ours is at least
You haunt our separation because it was my dependency

I know you talk about me
in the pits of your unconscious mind, I lie there in the same breath
we held together up the mountains
I know you think about me
in the morning of the schooldays when our classes are not our forte
Because you could never let go of this face

I know my memory feels very raw

like unsavoury meat, like unbitten flesh, I know I cause you distraught

Sunning up the city with no blues caught

You know the alter is false

yet you worship for my presence like a dog waiting to get his last meal

from the un-god knowing it was you the devil contract was bought

and I'll watch the sparrows at my window

leave their nest, in regret

you'll watch my tears slip away like cold mines on sunrise

The tabletop has your fruit on it

let's be clear, are you being honest?

I never dare to touch you with a finger but you said I scared you with

a knife.

what a foolish guy,

you lie about us to everyone else keying the lock to my frustration

knowing I'm painting your absence like a lost situation

ship, and it has sunk in the sea

you had fins and a tail

but you didn't bother to save me

you were scared of us maybe you still are

so I'll watch the sparrows

abandon their nest

like the last time you walked out of my car

the empty pen snapped

the scribbles were entertaining my destiny

and I've reached the synagogue

that I had sworn to leave in ruins

I walk past the violet walls coating them red with my Blood The lilac

sea is scarlet now The sky has already burned

now I watch by the minute the disgust of my heart

to heal something insatiable like a pin to a dart

the fruit will rot to summer it is mango season anyway Its the casket

lost

lost to the graveyard of fate

I hope when you left for the train the station was bustling with my

thoughts and yet you sat alone

Besides my absence like a walk

it'll be June once more,

the hills will flower the dead the mists will become death

and our memories will become unsaid

I don't think you deserve my kind words

these lines with golden ink rust not understanding the difference

between your love and unjust

and regardless I'm proud of you because it's the year '96

and the prophecy is done

and you're just one step closer to being

the one you promised to must

I loved you, so I drank tea from the raw clay pot. Guzzled your denial

down my throat like ancient poison, but for you, I swallowed it like

the tincture of touch.

I felt my bones become stone like the pot was carved from Medusa's

curse and

even though I lived, I carried the weight of my skull through my skin

and tendons.

And you ripped those apart with your jaws anchored with the venom

of a thousand false promises.

And now I am but flesh, standing beyond your naked sight. Trying to

flame the ceramics into my bones, trying to crock my tendons.

Trying to sew it all together with your absence. while you hold the needle,

with no anaesthesia,

and I still look at you like you're god

As you eat me alive just to turn me into a sculpture, a skeuomorph of your inability to love.

I resisted you

because my hands were stained with blood I shed in front of you of a war we fought together

and today I colour my room

my shade lost from the first war recollecting pieces from last summer rotting the muted hues of before

You walked along me for this epoch you speared the spear in my heart you spared me the misery

you changed the past

And I'm waiting for 6:30

waiting to wander around words waiting to figure out what's left to change the foreboding curse

I burnt my hair to be grotesque, while my friends anointed my mirror. I see you in the maroons of the black neighbourhood wither. You look the same and have the same face. But I'm what's different. The lack of me in your name. Son of the hunt sees us still, together in a haze of our past, I just wanted something to last. Too fast? Four Months down in the drain, you said you don't feel the same, and you still see me in your hurricane. Your worst nightmare, your best mate.

I wonder if your heart sinks again, hanging out with my ex-best friend. Becoming another mirage to your name. But do you go in a blurry haze? When you see my face? Every blue moon, even on my god's birthday? I wonder if you believe in god, to rid me of your taunts. You ever-lasting scarlet haunts.

The green and orange months, coming to the same end, last October all over again.

58. Trail

the trail of my love

knots itself around my ribs

my chest becomes more of a cage than my homeland already knew

I could write sonnets

on the margins of my bones, I have moths in my lungs

I wish my mother knew

It feels like yesterday was doomsday And tomorrow will be armageddon

I wish I could be a boy like all the boys but in my case, the gods have a say

Will my poetry become buried

or will it be like the spear that's in my chest

the wound so open, the flesh so rotten and my name ever so forgotten

When it's all over

I hope the stars remember there was me and there was no one else,

and how it was the greatest tragedy

59. Dreams

I have these dreams where I look at you, and we just stare at each other unsaid. Your face disrupts and merges into your iris, and there are no words, no constraints. The look of your eyes confesses everything: your hate, Your Heart, your disappointment, my betrayal.

And the lack of forgiveness and the beguiling the apostles of apologies. The Prime Meridian shifts a notch every time your eyes quiver to me. We don't always meet in a dream; we meet in the hallways, on stairs, beneath the roadside by the mall, in the neighbourhood, in the nocturnal hours of eternity. We meet every other day in this citywide town.

It makes me feel that if the streets lead to your residence, why do I try so hard to carve a new path? Maybe once more, I should walk to our home and make sure there are more memories in the garden than graves

60. Can't Betray God

I wake up with dust in my eyes, with the light of your discarding of me travelling through the crooked window. there's no god anymore, there's no way to betray her either. So why is my revenge so pitiful? your betrayal is like another piece of the puzzle I never wanted to complete. your betrayal reeks of despondent guilt. And it can't hurt me, nothing can hurt me more than my own self, nothing shrivels through my skin sharper than my catering to my casket.
My apologies only go so far. they won't heal any wounds, won't caster no minds, won't make anyone feel anything enough.

Every song I dedicated to my suffering has your vision in it because child. I was an infection that wanted your infancy, I was a wilt that needed the flowers of your need. I was withered by the time I was nine, and to make you wither became my destiny.
and this sunshine weather had made promises to me, to mould you into another version of me and would turn you into an apology, the sacrifice to the now dead gods. Who require feasts of foretold scrutiny. And I cut you up like a lamb and boiled you in the altar of Absence, Even the Heretic's Chapel would've called me a god the way I was willing to give up everything up for everyone, but in the constant construction between the constraints of wanting the world to be okay, and wanting you to be okay, and wanting you. I think I lost everything.
There was no god other than me, I buried you alive with the phantoms of my ex-best friend's mother's depression tea.

I was once told to choose between The world, My lover, And Their love. And in the spite of losing my subtleties that keep me alive. I saved none.

61. Petty Poison

I drank the petty poison to kill the boy who writes poems about you, I discarded the desolation of my sanity over undeserving people, you said so yourself. and the flesh is mine to scar. so I'll hoop onto new land and new shores and new muses and new hopes to figure out what the incandescent lights at the end of the un-dawning light have become, And I'll get over us. the ending world will bloom something new, and I'll become something more than your escapade.

62. How Do I Explain

You sit in my mind idle now, before you used to see the walls, cut the bones of my heart's slammer. wind up on the floor with your overgrown nails which I always envied.

And you say not to write poems about you, And my mind says don't do it. Don't write about someone who's been in contempt with my soul's symphonies. But It's restless.

You moved in my mind garden restless like an injured hog and now you sit there on the bench staring at me.

Why can't you just walk out? Why can't I just walk out? This Garden Of Ethos has no place for either of us.

I watch the tailorbird make a nest, and it lays its eggs. and you just sit breaking the fourth wall of my mind. You confuse me.

How do I explain that I'm haunted by the reminder of you, even when you're nothing to me? I don't feel your absence, I just feel your existence.

63. Somber Day

The somber day will come and this magnificent night will dwell down the sorrow that is of tomorrow, I will break apart my esteem to follow myself to my own grave, and the shovel made of gold will wither out. I'll banish myself to a new world that's yet again to be destroyed by my grief. In the essence of perfecting the nuisances of this crooked kingdom, I'll become the first wall of Vijayanagar to fall.

And I'll fall to my knees as the messiah who died a year after sixteen; knowing the last visit of mine was to the Musket Mortuary, where I picked up the ashes mixed with gunpowder and shot the nearest bits of my bitter accountability. Take me out, I'm tired of this ruined city.

64. Affair With Death

The staircase is infinite, And I roll down it so steep like a cliff and it bruises me everywhere people don't set their sight on, every cut is in the tunnels of their abandonment. and in this rigid invisible turmoil fragments my essence of mortality. I have this affair with death, I catch glimpses of her scythe cutting my time, time and time again. Feels like this lingering moment that might close, and the cliff stairs become steeper and steeper. It's pissing me off, The universe has a will and i'm its favourite experiment. but when i say god has no morals Im an abomination. A messiah Massacred by both god and its people, Why is that I see death in my mirror and everyone sees Armageddon in my eyes. If it's the end of the world with my death then why do you want me to die, and if my death is senseless why do you find ecstasy in my suffering. I make amends, I make my heart heard. and all you do, is stay violently silent. In this room, why is my breath the heaviest sound?

65. Recited

march back to the passive status of being alone with no one to sneak in through the window. the only thing that can climb through these iron bars is the spirit of absence. It lurks in the metal through which bleeds like mercury in my veins

Because luck is such a mercurial mercy, the only way I can ever strike a chord in tune is when happiness is being used as bait for my severity towards the supernatural.

But they have their name recited on my guitar that I don't even play, I'm a drummer, aren't I? I keep making a band out of my own bastion of nuances. And the juncture of my commitment to my own craft feels like a landmine I can't stop kicking.

I wanted to be a heretic to the womb goddess and I ended up being an infidel to her. Showing her that I could be a traitor was not enough, I had to make a new god.

66. Sanity

my sanity is limited, beyond the brink of my tolerance. It's just easier to show you're pulling water from the empty well, even if you're pulling up dirt. It's a culture of ambiguous Labour and your problems are ironically irrelevant until your labour is overwhelmingly visible.

67. How Do you?

How do you remove the need for love from yourself
when it's the one thing you're made of
when it's the one thing you're made for
how do you wretch out your wires
that circuit you the need of comfort
how do you stitch down revelations
that the one thing you crave
is not yours.

68. My Muse

I cave into my spine to make room for your reason of relevance. I despise you as my muse, I shrivel the shallows that cue your presence, I ignore my vision when you're in sentience. why now? why isn't your grave permanent? why isn't your intolerance my reason enough to leave you in the depths of the mortuary made of marine metaphors? Because the white and black bettas have lost their fins because all their gills could absorb were taunts given by the lack of a bright moon.

Why can't you just be this distant memory I forsake to the rhythm of my risk? why can't you, just be a person lost in the cold lilac mist?

69. Charade

And I look at myself with every last ounce of will, why is everything
stolen from me to the extent that I feel like the thief for holding onto
the lightest of likings?
I see this grace tumbling down the window that humbled my widowed
heart laden with rusted glass and cracked metal.
I feel this instant riddle that I need to solve to make sure someone
doesn't lose their life to the armageddon of arrogance, like the same
saviour complex messiah that couldn't even save the world,
Spirits says it's okay, to fail.
But manslaughter is still a drunk drive away from jail
Isn't addiction also a mistake? a complicit fail?
but you can only pick up your loss as long as it's not frail.
And it'll be okay to make mistakes
as long as you're the victim of your charade

70. Pedestal

and I stand tall over the towering pedestal made of thin ice, watch the cracks trace the shapes of my veins, and succumb to the misery of my irresponsibility. I keep making the same mistakes, driving into my own demise. the cracks start to sharpen with each road I take that I didn't choose. The lightning strikes through the compartment where I rest my flesh, one that barely belongs to me. To find solace on a road less taken, a road with corpses so many it might as well be a mortuary. And I have to compose my death in a way that serves others, compose my misery into a compulsion to be validated. because I am starved for wanting something that's about me. I am starved for comfort that doesn't come from being a hero. I am starved for love that comes my way because I can be loved and not that I need to prove my loyalty to every inch of the eldritch universe.

71. Court

Why am I found guilty of every sin I have yet to commit? always accounted for a trial in the court of kings just to be the blacksmith who crafts his own executioner's guillotine. And I wait for the day this decapitation finds a head to honour. I want my wings of wax to be made with some stature, and to have a gold spark in my eyes. But the lush blue of my life's hue has kept me at bay, finding ways to be wanted even when abandonment is the only truth that stands beyond this tall grass that worships my sin. the blades run through my skin like clay etched with ancient tales. but the world had ended. No one will find my corpse and kindle to my story. The forbidden flames will exorcise me or the Freezing abandonment will justify me.

72. In our Destiny

it's in our destiny for love to not exist in a form we can have it in, so please speak to me some time because the silence of your wounded tongue makes me bleed.

my ring finger has pretty nails that grew out to not be bitten, and look tidy and clean. I don't pay attention to it a lot. my task of letting go of you brings you closer to me, my will to be absent in your existence crafts your metaphors into my anatomy.

You're burning me by being too bright, and you're blinding the eyeless mime. You're such a beautiful monster. You're such a disgraced Divine.

73. Seeping Through Soil

But in the end, am I not the poison seeping through this soil? growing cascades of bones and bridges over the silhouettes of those who don't even breathe.

I can make death feel death but I cannot give divine to the god.

74. Harlot

The sanctity of my love is being demolished by each second, I turn into the Harboured Harlot at the bay of beguiling. The curse will never end, But should I? god, how desperately i want to touch the rotten skies, but no.

Stay Suraci, Feel the Fragments of the glass shards raining into your hourglass. Let your time crack, let the sand seep into the shore so your curse stays forever more.

Because you want this to be your life, relentless restlessness, rapid ropes leashing your legs to the crowd that taunts you more.

I'm not a harlot. I'm a Sailor. And you don't understand why the womb goddess hates us. I wish to be taller, so at least my lack of strength will make me a care gaoler

75. Blacksmith (Saif Madre)

you want to feel loved child,

but the same same thing that hones you, consumes you. you can cut through all the bones and tear through all the tendons yet you won't be rid of these feelings. your pain is an accessory, not the bridge to escape. this love that you once tasted as a casual treat turned out to be a cruel casualty. it runs deeper than your bones, farther than the edge of the blade can reach. you can't wiggle it out of your skin or drown it with your blood, it runs through the ridges of your brain and kisses your soul every fortnight. you can run from it but your Achilles heel is bruised and you can't jump over the potholes you dug yourself. you are bound to fall, just as you fell for love.

your lover awaits you, or so you think. your lover is at the window, longing for your presence, yearning for the light you don't know you carry. they whisper sweet nothings but you have bullets lodged in your skull, you fail to mention you were holding the gun yourself. your silence is an answer to all the questions brimming in the air. are you scared? the worry lines on your forehead gleam with the sweat. are you tired too? rest the night. your lover will still await you. or so you think.

76. Reserved

I want to be loved but I know all the love I want is reserved for those who hurt me, I know the world has ended and I've forgiven and grieved for the one I loved but my tensed wings clench with the reminder that the love was not two way, not enough at-least...

Epilogue

They never told you the tale of Aksara.

Not in the sermons of the Womb Goddess, not in the chants of the Covenant, not even in the drunken confessions of prophets who forgot the taste of silence.

She was the daughter of Agandeviyan, born not of womb but of word. They say she was carved from the syllables of a prayer too long to remember, too desperate to forget. Where others inherited blood, she inherited echoes.

Aksara walked where the storm had not yet touched, on the edges of the Lilac Sea, her steps weaving hymns into the foam. The gods looked upon her and grew uneasy, for she carried no prophecy, no chain of fate, no debt of sacrifice. She was, in truth, unwritten.

And in a world that fed upon destiny, the unwritten child was the most dangerous of all.

When Suraci's failure turned the sky violet and the world collapsed into fragments, Aksara did not mourn. She did not curse the gods or kneel to Moherani. Instead, she whispered into the storm. And for the first time, the storm listened.

They say her voice became a second sky, not to shield, not to save, but to remind creation that even ruins can sing.

The story ends not with Suraci's storm, but with Aksara's silence, an unfinished sentence, waiting still.

Codex Of The Shattered World

I. Death and Its Layers

Death in this world is not singular, but layered.

Lesser Deaths: Countless shadows roam, each responsible for small endings. They take the death of a bird, the collapse of a house, or the fading of a memory. These are called The Pale Host.

Greater Deaths: Abstract entities that claim entire cities, nations, or even ages. Their names are forgotten, for to speak them is to invite endings.

Moherani, The First Death: The origin and ruler of all deaths. She alone can take what is eternal, what cannot be touched by decay. Only Moherani can unmake the undying.

Mortality is layered. A pebble is taken by a minor death, a king by a greater death, but a god only by Moherani herself.

II. Paradox Gods

In the Shattered World, gods cannot exist without contradiction. Their essence is formed from two irreconcilable truths bound into one body. This is why their power is immense but also unstable.

Agandeviyan: The Purifying Flame that both heals and devours, paradox eternal. His hunger was sharpened when he swallowed the river-goddess Ganga, making fire drink water and still burn.

Womb Goddess: Creator yet Abandoner. She births life but rejects her children, proving that creation itself can be cruelty.

Moherani: The Death that cannot die. An ending that continues endlessly.

Paradoxes sustain divinity, but they also make the gods brittle. What sustains them can also collapse them.

III. *The Four Storms*

When Suraci failed, the storm did not remain one. It split the world into four great halves, each ruled by its own fragment of the storm.

Western Storm: The land Suraci wanders, filled with lilac skies and fractured seas.

Eastern Storm: Shards of forgotten gods howl here, and faith has become madness.

Northern Storm: Frozen in violet lightning, where time fractures and never heals.

Southern Storm: A furnace of ash and rain, where Agandeviyan's fire still licks the earth.

These four halves never touch. They spiral around each other like drifting continents caught in eternal weather.

IV. *Wild Magic*

The storm brewed more than ruin. It spilled wild magic into the cracks of reality.

Wild magic is untamed creation, raw and formless, leaking from the paradoxes of the gods.

It warps mortals, creating half-beasts, dream-echoes, and storms of memory.

Some call it divine mercy, others call it curse, but none can control it. Wild magic moves as the storm moves, unbound and unfathomable.

V. The Ban on the Birth of New Gods

A cosmic law binds the heavens. No new god can be born while Suraci lives.

This law is not mercy. It is punishment. Suraci's survival keeps the cycle incomplete and locks creation in stasis.

The gods cannot give birth, the world cannot heal, the storm cannot close.

His existence is both anchor and prison. If he dies, the world may collapse utterly. If he lives, the storm never ends.

For this reason mortals whisper that Suraci is not a savior, but the final chain that binds eternity.

Would you like me to also rewrite the earlier epilogue about Aksara in the same codex-like tone without em dashes, so it flows consistently with this?

A cosmic law binds the heavens: no new god can be born while Suraci lives.

This is not mercy, it is punishment. Suraci's survival keeps the cycle incomplete, locking creation in stasis.

The gods cannot birth, the world cannot heal, the storm cannot close.

His existence is both anchor and prison: if he dies, the world may collapse utterly. If he lives, the storm never ends.
Thus, mortals whisper that Suraci is not a savior, but the final chain keeping eternity bound.